ch

WHIZZY SCIENCE

Make it SPLASH!

Written by:
Anna Claybourne

Illustrated by:
Kimberley Scott and Venetia Dean

First published in 2013 by Wayland
Copyright © Wayland 2013

Wayland
338 Euston Road
London NW1 3BH

Wayland Australia
Hachette Children's Books
Level 17/207
Kent Street
Sydney, NSW 2000

Senior Editor: Julia Adams
Editor: Annabel Stones
Designer: Anthony Hannant (LittleRedAnt)
Illustrator (step-by-steps): Kimberley Scott
Illustrator (incidentals and final crafts): Venetia Dean
Proofreader & Indexer: Sara Harper

The website addresses (URLs) included in this book were valid at the time of going to press. However, it is possible that contents or addresses may have changed since the publication of this book. No responsibility for any such changes can be accepted by either the author or the Publisher.

Dewey categorisation: 530.4'2
ISBN 978 0 7502 7735 8

Printed in China

Wayland is a division of Hachette Children's Books,
an Hachette UK company.

www.hachette.co.uk

Picture acknowledgements:
All photographs: Shutterstock
except: p. 13 (bottom): NASA/DVIDS Hub; p. 27 (bottom):
AlejandroLinaresGarcia/Wikipedia.

Contents

SPLASH!

In everyday life, we're surrounded by liquids all the time. Water falls on our heads as rain, makes up most of our drinks, and fills our rivers and lakes, baths and swimming pools. Then there's runny paint and glue, cooking oil, and the liquid fuels that make cars and aircraft work.

SPLOSH

SQUEEZE

DRIP, DRIP

SPLAT

WHAT IS A LIQUID?

Along with solids and gases, liquids are one of the three states of matter – forms that substances can exist in depending on how hot or cold they are. For example, on our planet, water is usually found as a liquid, but it can also be a solid (ice), and a gas (water vapour), which is found in the air.

DRIP, DRIP

Solid   Liquid   Gas

LIKE A LIQUID

Liquids can do things that solids and gases can't. Solids tend to stay the same shape. Gases spread out to fill the space they are in. But a liquid moves in a different way. You can pour a liquid, make waves in it, or paint with it. Liquids can flow, spill, squirt, soak and SPLASH!

WATER OF LIFE

For us, water is the most important liquid of all. Living things need liquid water to survive. In fact, we only exist because the Earth is mostly at the right temperature for water to exist as a liquid.

TWEET TWEET

PITTER

PATTER

LIQUID SCIENCE

This book is bursting with splashy, soggy experiments that will help you find out all kinds of cool things about liquids. To experiment like a real scientist, remember these tips:

• Follow all the instructions carefully.

• Watch closely to see what happens, and try to record your results in writing or photos.

• If you can, do experiments more than once to see if they always work in the same way.

SPLASH

Make a Splash

Experiment with how liquids splash using these simple, yet messy tests. It might be best to do them outdoors!

YOU WILL NEED

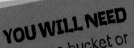

1) A large bucket or washing-up bowl
2) Water
3) Waterproof household objects, like pebbles, buttons, coins or fruit
4) Small plastic bowls or yoghurt pots
5) Runny paint
6) Large pieces of plain paper or newspaper
7) A plastic cup
8) A tray

Here's What to Do...

1. Half-fill your bowl or bucket with water, and drop different objects into it. Which things make the biggest and smallest splashes?

2. Stand a small bowl of paint in the middle of a large piece of paper. Make splash art by dropping a pebble into the paint.

3. Fill a plastic cup to the brim with water and stand it on a tray. Then hold the tray in one hand, stretch out your arm, and try walking a distance of 6 m without spilling any water.

6

WHAT'S GOING ON?

When you disturb a liquid, it moves around in waves and ripples, or separates into droplets – tiny 'pieces' of liquid. Droplets form a ball shape, because liquid likes to cling to itself. Heavier, lumpier objects make a bigger splash because they push more liquid out of the way. Light, smooth or thin objects make less of a splash, as they move less water.

! TROUBLESHOOTER

If you do want to do these indoors, put down LOTS of newspaper or plastic mats and wear an apron.

PLOP!

See if you can capture a splash on video or as a freeze-frame photo.

WHAT NEXT?

Try test number three as a race with two or more friends, each with their own tray and cup. Who can keep the most water in their cup?

7

stretchy water Skin

Why does water seem to have a stretchy skin?

YOU WILL NEED

1) A large plastic bowl
2) Water
3) Metal sewing pins and needles
4) Liquid soap (hand wash or washing-up liquid)

Here's What to Do...

1. Fill the bowl with water almost to the top and let it settle to a calm, still surface.

2. Drop a pin or needle into the water from above the surface – it should sink, as metal is denser (heavier for its size) than water.

3. Then try gently placing a pin or needle onto the surface and see if you can get it to lie on top.

4. Add a drop of liquid soap to the water. What happens?

WHAT'S GOING ON?

Water doesn't actually have a skin, but it seems to. This is because the molecules in water pull towards each other, especially at the surface. This makes a kind of stretchy barrier called surface tension. Soapy chemicals break the pull between the molecules, and destroy the surface tension.

 You might also be able to make pepper grains, or even a paper clip or safety pin, lie on the surface.

TROUBLESHOOTER

If you have trouble making things stay on the surface, try using tweezers to put them on, or lie them on a piece of tissue paper on the water. The paper will soak up water and sink, leaving the pins or needles behind.

Some water insects such as pond skaters and whirligig beetles use surface tension to skate along on top of the water.

WHAT NEXT?

Fill a small glass with water to the brim, then drop in pins to make it fuller and fuller. How many can you add before it overflows? Surface tension makes the water bulge out over the top of the glass.

Upside-down CUP

This experiment also makes an amazing magic trick! Do it outdoors or over a large water tray, just in case.

YOU WILL NEED
1) A handkerchief or any piece of thin fabric
2) A small glass
3) A jug of water

Here's What to Do...

1. Put your handkerchief or fabric over the glass and hold it loosely in place.

2. Carefully pour water through the fabric into the glass, until it's almost full.

3. Put your hand around the glass and pull the fabric down so that it's stretched tightly across the top of the glass.

4. Put your other hand over the glass and turn it upside down.

5. Then – ta-daa! – gently take your hand away. The water doesn't fall out!

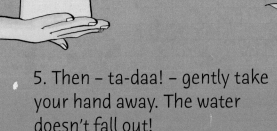

WHAT'S GOING ON?

When the water is flowing and the fabric can move and ripple, the surface tension is broken and the water gets through. When the glass is upside down, the water's surface tension forms a barrier across each tiny hole in the smooth, flat, tightly stretched fabric.

TROUBLESHOOTER

The fabric must be stretched smooth and tight for it to work.

WATERPROOF SKIN

Tents and umbrellas often use surface tension to keep water out. When the fabric is stretched tight, it can get covered in rain, but the rain doesn't come through, even if the fabric isn't waterproof. Instead the surface tension makes the water 'block' all the tiny holes in the fabric.

WHAT NEXT?

You can do a similar trick by placing a postcard on top of a brim-full cup of water. Hold it on, turn the cup upside down, then let go. The card forms a barrier that doesn't let air in, so water can't fall out because there is no air to replace it.

Water balloon POP

If you fill a balloon with water, what does the water inside it look like? Find out by taking a photo! You need at least two people.

Here's What to Do...

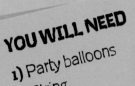

YOU WILL NEED

1) Party balloons
2) String
3) A pin or needle
4) A camera or cameraphone

1. Fill several party balloons with water and tie them closed.

2. Use string to hang the balloons up on a washing line, low tree branch or something similar, outdoors! If there's nothing suitable to hang them on, ask someone to stand and hold the string.

3. One person should pop a balloon with a pin.

4. At the moment of popping, another person should take a photo of the balloon. Use the fastest shutter speed possible or set the camera to 'action' mode.

12

WHAT'S GOING ON?

It may take a few tries to get a good photo (that's why you need several balloons!) – but if you're lucky you will capture a balloon-shaped ball of water hanging in mid-air after the balloon pops. The stretchy balloon skin shrinks so fast that it leaves the water uncovered before gravity pulls it to the ground.

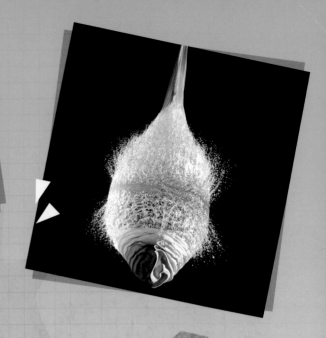

! TROUBLESHOOTER

Count 3, 2, 1, pop! to get the timing as exact as possible.

SPACE BALLOON

Astronauts have also done this experiment in space, where it's easier to get a good look!

WHAT NEXT?

You could try videoing the pop, then playing back the film slowed down to see what happens. You could even ask someone to try to catch the water ball as it falls, for an extra splashy photo!

Things that float

Try this experiment to find out what things float in water, and why.

YOU WILL NEED

1) A large mixing or washing-up bowl
2) Water
3) A selection of everyday objects
4) Modelling clay

Here's What to Do...

1. Half-fill the large bowl with water.

2. Put different objects in it to see what floats and what doesn't.

OBJECTS TO TRY

Coin Paper clip Chocolate Seashell
Pebble Cork Eraser Buttons Toys
Balls Wooden pegs

Can you guess which ones will float before you put them in?

3. Make a round ball of modelling clay – it should sink.

4. Can you make the clay into a shape that floats, even though it is a material that sinks?

14

WHAT'S GOING ON?

Water can hold up any object that is less dense than itself. Density means how heavy an object is for its size. A coin is small and quite dense. It sinks because it is heavier than an amount of water of the same size and shape, and the water cannot hold it up. A cork is much less dense. It pushes down into the water a little, but the water can easily hold it up.

Modelling clay is dense and doesn't float. But if you make a boat or cup shape out of the clay, it does! This is because the shape now includes the air inside it. Taken together, the air and the clay make an object that is less dense than water.

BIG BOATS

Huge ocean ships are made of metal and are very heavy – but they float because of all the air inside them.

WHAT NEXT?

Can you find any natural boat shapes, such as bottle tops or fruit skins? See if they float.

Try to build a boat that moves – could you add a small sail and make wind with a straw?

Rising raisins

Amaze your friends with raisins that float, then sink, then float again!

Here's What to Do...

YOU WILL NEED
1) A few raisins
2) Fizzy water or a clear fizzy drink, such as lemonade
3) A tall glass
4) A stopwatch

1. Fill the glass with the fizzy drink, almost to the top.

2. Drop a raisin into the drink and watch it sink to the bottom.

3. Wait a minute or two. What happens?

4. How long will your raisin keep rising and sinking? See if you can time it.

WHAT'S GOING ON?

The raisin is denser than the drink, so at first it sinks. But as it sits in the fizzy liquid, gas bubbles from the drink start to get stuck to the raisin's rough surface. Eventually, it has so many bubbles on it that it becomes lighter and less dense, so it floats. But when it reaches the surface, the bubbles escape into the air. Without its bubbles, the raisin sinks back to the bottom – and the cycle begins again!

TROUBLESHOOTER

You need a really bubbly, freshly opened fizzy drink, not an old one.

FROM FIZZY TO FLAT

If you leave a fizzy drink in a glass, eventually all the gas bubbles will escape from it, and it will go 'flat'. Once this happens, the raisin will stop moving.

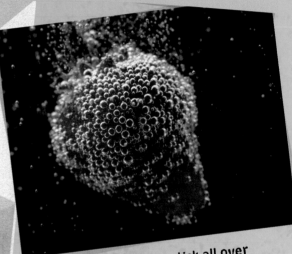

Bubbles of gas stick all over the surface of objects dropped into fizzy drinks.

WHAT NEXT?

Try the same experiment with other objects like popcorn, paper clips, small sweets or pasta shapes. Do any of them behave the same way? Do any of them stay at the bottom of the drink, or stay floating on the top? Do they get soggy?

17

Magic liquid levels

It's not just solid objects that float on liquids – other liquids do too.

YOU WILL NEED

1) A tall, clear glass, jam jar
2) A measuring jug
3) 6 paper cups
4) 100 ml (half a cup) each of runny honey, maple syrup, washing-up liquid, milk, cooking oil (such as sunflower oil) and water

1. Measure out your six liquids into the six paper cups, using the measuring jug.

2. Pour the honey into the bottom of your jar.

3. Add the other liquids one by one, pouring them slowly and carefully into the middle so they don't stick to the sides.

4. Let the liquids settle. What happens?

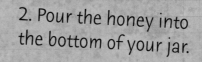

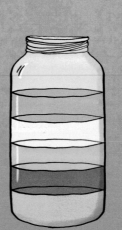

18

WHAT'S GOING ON?

As you pour them in, the densest liquids sink down, and the less dense liquids rise up and float on top of them, creating a stripy tower of different layers. Scientists call this a density column.

Remember not to drink this mixture – it's not food!

TROUBLESHOOTER

Try to choose liquids of different colours, such as bright pink or green washing-up liquid and golden honey. You could also add some food colouring to the water in the paper cup, to make it easier to see.

OIL ON WATER

Oil is less dense than water and floats on top of it. That's why oil spills at sea are bad news. The oil sits on the water surface, forming an oil slick, and making water birds' feathers dirty and sticky.

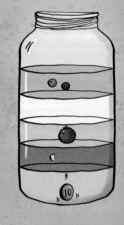

WHAT NEXT?

Now try dropping in some small objects to see if they float on top, sink to the bottom or stop somewhere in the middle. Try a coin, popcorn kernel or sunflower seed, plastic beads, a small tomato or a toy brick.

Melting Crayon art

Solids can become liquids when they get hot and melt. You can sometimes see this happening with ice and snow, butter or chocolate – and in this experiment, wax crayons.

Here's What to Do...

1. Tape the crayons pointing downwards to a big piece of card, like this.

2. Get someone to hold the card up vertically.

3. Ask an adult to plug in and switch on the hairdryer, and use it to blast the crayons with hot air.

4. As the crayons start to melt, the person holding the card can tip and tilt it to make patterns.

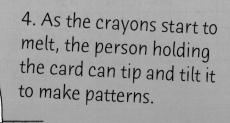

WHAT'S GOING ON?

When the crayons are solid they hold their shape. But when the heat melts them they become a liquid and start to flow, so gravity can pull them downwards. By tipping and tilting the card, you can make the wax flow into all kinds of crazy patterns.

Solid   **Solid/Liquid**   **Liquid**

The solid ice becomes a liquid, water, when it melts.

TROUBLESHOOTER

You can use brown card from a large cardboard box if you don't have white card.

MULTICOLOURED CRAYONS

To make multicoloured crayons, peel the paper off a few crayons and put them in a paper cup. Heat the cup with the hairdryer until they have melted then swirl them together with a stick. Leave the mix to cool and harden, then pop out!

WHAT NEXT?

For a shiny version, cover your card with silver foil before you stick the crayons on.

The saliva test

Did you know that food has to be dissolved in liquid before you can taste it? Try this test to find out how important your saliva (spit) is!

Here's What to Do...

YOU WILL NEED

1) Some strong-tasting foods, such as salty crisps and sweet dried apricots, or a few grains of salt and sugar

2) Paper or plastic plates

3) Kitchen paper

1. Set out your foods on separate plates.

2. Stick your tongue out and dab a bit of each food onto it. You should be able to taste them straight away.

3. Now dry your tongue all over with kitchen paper.

4. Dab the foods on your tongue again. Is there any difference?

22

WHAT'S GOING ON?

Your tongue has taste-sensing taste buds in it, but they are in tiny cracks in the tongue's surface. For food to reach them, it has to be washed down into the cracks. Your tongue is normally wet because your mouth constantly releases saliva. As soon as the saliva touches food, it dissolves some of it and washes it down the gaps. When your tongue is totally dry, this can't happen and you can't taste anything.

TROUBLESHOOTER

You need to use foods that are quite dry, so avoid juicy fruit or yoghurt.

WE NEED SPIT

Saliva has other uses, too. It helps to make food mushy and soft, so it's easier to swallow. It can also kill some types of germs.

WHAT NEXT?

Chocolate is designed to stay solid until it's in your mouth, when it melts into a liquid. Try putting some squares of chocolate in the freezer, then compare them with unfrozen squares. What happens when you put them in your mouth? Can you taste the unfrozen squares sooner?

Make your own river

Though water seems soft, it can cut a path through sand, soil or solid rock. That's how rivers form.

YOU WILL NEED

1) Plenty of play sand (available at garden centres)

2) A large, shallow tray that can get wet and dirty

3) Pebbles of various sizes

4) A garden hose or a large jug of water

Here's What to Do...

1. Find somewhere safe outdoors to put the tray, where it's OK to spill water and sand.

2. Use the sand and a few pebbles to build a gently sloping hillside in the tray, with the top of the hill at one end. Pack the sand down firmly.

3. Use the garden hose or water jug to pour a slow, steady trickle of water onto the top of your hill.

4. Watch as the water finds its way downhill and carves itself a river bed.

WHAT'S GOING ON?

As gravity pulls the water downwards, it finds the easiest path, flowing around harder areas and blockages. As the water flows, it washes away some sand, creating a channel which gets bigger and bigger as more water flows along it.

TROUBLESHOOTER

You want the water to flow away off the tray once it reaches the other end, so don't use a deep tray.

RIVERS AND ROCKS

Rivers cut through sand easily, but they can also wear through rock, though this takes much longer. The water gradually dissolves the rock as it flows along, and sand and pebbles carried along in the water also wear it away.

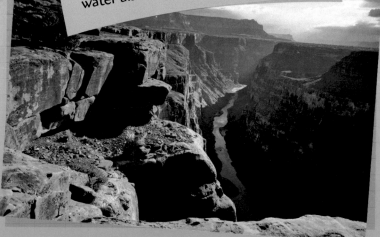

WHAT NEXT?

Look at maps or satellite pictures (for example, of the Nile in Egypt or the Irtysh River in Russia), or even at real rivers next time you're in a high-up place or on board a plane, to see how their paths have formed.

You could also do this activity on a sandy beach without a tray. Just build a sandy, pebbly hill and pour water down it.

strange gloop

Some strange liquids don't behave quite the way you expect! Do this experiment outside, or make sure you put down lots of newspaper.

YOU WILL NEED

1) A packet of cornflour, also called cornstarch or maize flour
2) A large mixing bowl
3) Water
4) A cup
5) A spoon

Here's What to Do...

1. Put about a cupful of cornflour into the bowl.

2. Stir in a cupful of cold water, adding a little at a time until you have a gloopy liquid as thick as runny honey.

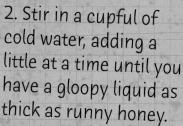

3. If you gently stir, pour or swirl the mixture, it's runny like a normal liquid.

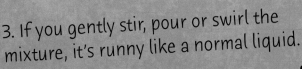

4. But what happens when you try to stir it quickly, or hit the surface hard with your hand?

WHAT'S GOING ON?

This mixture is called a non-Newtonian fluid, meaning it doesn't behave according to the normal laws of liquid science. When you are gentle with it, it flows and splashes. But when it's pushed hard, the particles in it jam together and form a lump, making it behave like a solid.

TROUBLESHOOTER

You may need to keep adding a little of both ingredients until you get the mixture just right.

HOLDING GLOOP

You might even be able to squeeze together a handful of the gloop into a ball, if you keep holding it tight. When you let go, it goes runny again!

WALKING ON GLOOP

Some experimenters have even tried filling a whole paddling pool with cornflour gloop to see if they could run across the surface. They could!

WHAT NEXT?

You can use a little green food colouring to turn your strange gloop into spooky slime!

More Water fun

Not quite soaked through yet? Here are some more amazing water tricks to try!

YOU WILL NEED

1) Water
2) A garden hose or spray bottle with a fine mist setting
3) 2 paper cups
4) String
5) Strong sticky tape
6) A kitchen or bathroom tap
7) An assistant to help you

Here's What to Do...

1. Make a rainbow
On a sunny day, stand with the sun behind you and spray a fine mist of water using a garden hose or spray bottle. A rainbow should appear in the misty water cloud.

2. Walking water
Tape a piece of string to the inside of the paper cup and ask your assistant to hold the cup still. Hold the string so that it slopes up diagonally out of the cup. Fill the other cup with water and slowly pour it out onto the end of string. It should travel along the string into the empty cup.

! TROUBLESHOOTER

The string will work best if you wet it first, but keep one end dry for taping.

3. String of pearls

Turn on a tap so that it is making a very thin, straight flow of water. Put your finger under the flow and lift it up close to the tap. Can you make the water form a series of tiny sphere shapes?

WHAT'S GOING ON?

The rainbow appears because as sunlight passes in and out of water droplets, it refracts or bends, and splits into separate colours.

The water 'walks' along the string because of a force called cohesion, which means sticking together. The water molecules cling to each other as they flow along the string, instead of dropping off it.

The string of pearls effect happens because there is such a small amount of water above your finger that surface tension tries to pull it into round droplets.

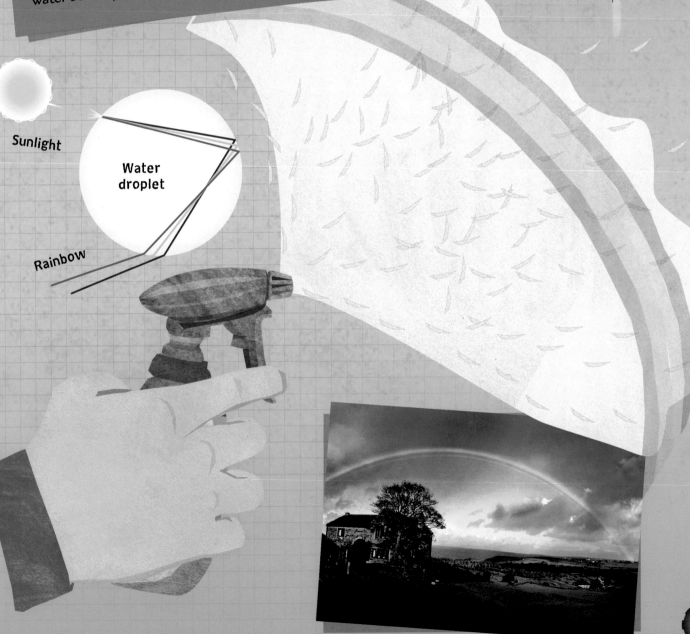

Sunlight

Water droplet

Rainbow

Glossary

cohesion Pulling or sticking together.

density How heavy a substance is compared to the space it takes up

density column A set of different liquids floating on top of each other.

dissolve To become mixed into a liquid and broken down into tiny parts.

droplet A tiny drop of liquid.

gas A state of matter in which a substance floats around freely.

liquid A state of matter in which a substance can flow and splash.

molecules Tiny units that make up substances.

non-Newtonian fluid A liquid that doesn't behave in a normal way.

oil slick Spilt oil floating on the surface of the sea.

refraction The way light bends when it moves from one clear substance into another.

saliva Another name for spit.

solid A state of matter in which a substance keeps its shape.

states of matter The forms that a substance can take: solid, liquid and gas.

surface tension The way molecules on the surface of water pull together and seem like a skin.

taste buds Tiny sense organs in the tongue that detect tastes.

water vapour Water in the form of a gas.

further reading

BOOKS

Experiments with Liquids
by Christine Taylor-Butler, Raintree, 2012

Experiments with Water
by Angela Royston, Franklin Watts, 2012

Solids, Liquids and Gases
by Louise and Richard Spilsbury, Raintree, 2013

The Science in: A Glass of Water
by Anna Claybourne, Franklin Watts, 2008

The Solid Truth about States of Matter with Max Axiom
by Agnieszka Biskup, Capstone Press, 2009

WEBSITES

Water Science for Kids
http://www.sciencekids.co.nz/water.html

Science Games for Kids: Solids, Liquids and Gases
http://www.sciencekids.co.nz/gamesactivities/gases.html

BBC Science Melting Activity
http://www.bbc.co.uk/schools/scienceclips/ages/8_9/solid_liquids.shtml

Index

Whizzy SCIENCE

Titles in the series:

Make it Zoom!
978 0 7502 7732 7

Zooming cars
Straw shooter
Heli-zoomer
Zero-gravity water squirt
Zooming balloon rocket
Magazine tug-of-war
Jelly slide
Flying bucket
Whirling wind speed meter
Ping pong flinger
Gas-fuelled rocket
Magnet power

Make it Bang!
978 0 7502 7731 0

See a bang
Bang, twang, pop!
How a bang travels
The speed of a bang
Bangs and whispers
The screaming cup
High and low
The sounds of speech
Solid sounds
Stop that banging!
Find the bang
How musical are you?

Make it Change!
978 0 7502 7734 1

Turn a penny green!
Lava volcano
The red cabbage test
Exploding drinks
Make salt disappear
  and reappear
Rubbery bones
Bottle balloon
Magic ice cubes
Plastic bag ice cream
Pure water still
Make your own butter
Mould garden

Make it Grow!
978 0 7502 7736 5

Egg-head!
Growing beans
Supermarket sprout!
Black bag balloon
Make a thermometer
Expanding ice
Sugary strings
Grow your own stalactites
Microwave a marshmallow
Popcorn!
Make bread rise
Squirty cream challenge

Make it Glow!
978 0 7502 7733 4

Light and shadows
Periscope
Tea light lanterns
Make an indoor rainbow
Glowing envelopes, plasters
  and sweets!
Glow-in-the-dark shapes
Make a glowing jar lantern
Glow stick photos
Glowing water stream
Laser jelly
Camera obscura
Ultraviolet glow

Make it Splash!
978 0 7502 7735 8

Make a splash
Stretchy water skin
Upside-down cup
Water balloon pop!
Things that float
Rising raisins
Magic liquid levels
Melted crayon art
The saliva test
Make your own river
Strange gloop
More water fun

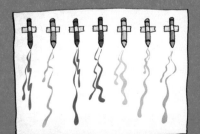